Pr
Corazón de agua / Heart of Water

"These are poems of both rootedness and transcendence, full of heart and breath and lift. Poems of river- and birdsong, there is a holy rustling here as 'wingbeats like sheets of paper' rise and lift."

— Kevin Rabas, Poet Laureate of Kansas (2017-2019), *While Away*

"The poems of *Corazón de agua / Heart of Water* validate the concretely visceral and alternately intangible impact of the last few years, the lonely individual experience and what's shared, concentrated tension between sensory deprivation and overload, appreciation of what went unnoticed before, coupled with dissociation and coping with grief."

— Jenny Irizary, Editor at Somos en escrito Literary Foundation Press

"Multilingual poet professor Xánath Caraza's new English and Spanish bilingual collection *Corazon de agua / Heart of Water* provides readers with her intimate sensorial observations in crisp elemental language expressed in mainly free verse. She captures cataloging almost-haiku-like topographical cycles of nature parallel to our human hearts' emotional fields of contraction and expansion. Close readers will also discover there's a boldface type contrapuntal poem interwoven in each poem.

"There are undercurrent references of what has become our modern plague's 'lockdown' appearing interwoven with strong seasonal biological and ecological cycles as in her poem 'The Origin of My Blood,' '…furrows are formed on my skin as black tears slide down. Distance is more painful with this unexpected pandemic' doing so while cognizant of our society's interdependence on people doing their jobs which Caraza celebrates and has concern for as in the poem 'Raven,' 'I think of those who travel on the metro every day, without masks, without distance between them, without knowing what they will become.'

"I found Caraza's new poems reminiscent of ecological-minded poets like Diana de Prima's early work on the natural world as well as Gary Snyder's mindfulness love of Nature rooted in Zen practice which she suggests in lines like in her title poem, 'I stir a memory to let it go. When invoked, it vanishes. I add the sighs provoked by the mares that gallop on the prairies. I imbibe the bright green, brilliant daybreak, heart of water.'"

— Carlos Cumpián, Author of *Human Cicada* (Prickly Pear Publishing)

Corazón de agua
Heart of Water

Corazón de agua / Heart of Water
Copyright © 2024
Published by Somos en escrito Literary Foundation Press
Berkeley, California
www.somosenescrito.com

Somos en escrito Literary Foundation Press retains copyright of the title, the front cover art and design, as well as the back cover design and all complementary text.

All rights reserved. No part of this book may be reprinted or reproduced or utilized in any form or by any electronic, mechanical, or other means, now known or hereafter invented, including photocopying and recording, or in any information storage or retrieval system, without permission in writing from the respective author, or from the publisher: Somos en escrito Literary Foundation Press, except in the case of brief quotations embodied in critical articles and reviews giving proper accreditation.

Disclaimer: The views, thoughts, and opinions expressed in the text belong solely to the author, and do not necessarily represent those of the Somos en escrito Literary Foundation.

Trademark notice: Product or corporate names may be trademarks or registered trademarks, and are used only for identification and explanation without intent to infringe.

Library of Congress Cataloging-in-Publication Data

A catalog record for this book has been requested

ISBN: 979-8-9902068-2-3

Typeset in Times New Roman

The Somos en escrito Literary Foundation is a small, independent Press that operates Somos en escrito Magazine and Somos en escrito Press, the book publishing unit: a tax-exempt, nonprofit organization, IRS Code number 81-3162209.

For any inquiries, write to Somos en escrito Literary Foundation Press at somosenescrito@gmail.com.

Cover: "Untitled" 1998 by Martha Caraza

Cover design: Luz Schweig

Corazón de agua
Heart of Water

by Xánath Caraza

Translated by Sandra Kingery

SOMOS EN ESCRITO

LITERARY FOUNDATION PRESS

BERKELEY

2024

Índice / Table of Contents

Prólogo / Foreword by Amy Sage Webb Baza   i

I. Corazón de agua / Heart of Water

Corazón de agua	3
Heart of Water	4

II. Un cardenal / A Cardinal

Nostalgia	7
Nostalgia	8
Esperanza	9
Hope	10
Confinamiento	11
Lockdown	13
Un cardenal	15
A Cardinal	16
Cada cuerpo	17
Each and Every Body	18
Una madre más nos deja	19
Another Mother Leaves Us	20
Con poesía	21
With Poetry	22

III. Cuervo / Raven

Efecto dominó	25
Domino Effect	26
Prestos a la vida	27
Prepared for Life	28
Punto de fuga	29
Vanishing Point	30
En la pantalla	31
On the Screen	32

El origen de mi sangre	33
The Origin of My Blood	34
En la rama	35
On the Branch	36
Cuervo	37
Raven	38

IV. Aliento / Breath

Se perchan en tus ráfagas	41
They Perch on Your Breezes	42
Elíxir	43
Elixir	44
Aliento	45
Inhalation	46
Magia	47
Magic	48
Canción de agua	49
Song of Water	50
La inevitable	51
Inevitable	52
Viaje	53
Journey	54
Canto helado	55
Frozen Song	56
Palabras	57
Words	58
Silencio	59
Silence	60
Lo que nos libera	61
What Frees Us	62
Pide agua	63
It Wants Water	64
Una llamarada en las ramas	65
A Blaze in the Branches	66
Invernales palabras	67

	Wintery Words	68
	Pensamientos ocultos	69
	Thoughts Concealed	70
	Sólo así	71
	The Only Way	72
V.	**Corazón de agua / Heart of Water**	
	Corazón de agua	75
	Heart of Water	76

Acknowledgments 79

About the Author 81

About the Translator 82

Foreword

These are poems of witness, bearing testament to the experience of the COVID-19 pandemic through the experience of self. To write as a poet of witness to the COVID-19 pandemic presents the distinct challenge of point of view. In sequestration, one's experience becomes intensely personal. Observations of others become masked and virtual. There is no vantage point from which to trace the shape or scale of what is transpiring.

These are meditative poems to be fully present for quotidian details during COVID, online and virtual life as glimpsed through a window, in stasis, and animated by the visitations of birds. These poems show our world reduced to windows and glimpses of things actual and virtual. The experience of suspended time creates an eternal presence, a timelessness and contemplation of the eternal. Within this stillness, these poems locate through perceptions of the elemental: wind, water, earth, fire, the sun/sunlight, and darkness.

A Buddhist practice of perceiving interconnectedness in all things, the farmer and the rain and the soil in each grain of rice, pervades these meditations. Caraza contemplates the way calamity makes precious the lives and work behind our own lives, all "those" to whom we are connected in each breath we take.

The repetition of sequestered days becomes its own form of meditation. Words and thoughts repeat throughout the collection, and within each poem bolded words create a type of haiku, a stilling and distillation of meaning. Each poem is fifteen lines of five tercets. The effect is something like an unrhymed Terza Rima Sonnet, except in the doldrums of pandemic quarantine; there is no certainty of a defining endpoint bringing any of the poems to summary in a couplet.

Rather, the final three lines carry each poem through its observation while opening to yet another day, another reach.

Intricate repetitions of words and images throughout these poems create a new form of sorts, something like a terzanelle meets sestina.

Caraza explores the effect of finding ourselves untethered from and separated from our sense of place, how we become increasingly aware of what we carry in the blood. We yearn for connection to the place of our birth. Denied means of traversing it, the distance we find ourselves from home places thrums in our blood.

Caraza bears witness to, meditates upon and offers redress for the insufficiency of isolated lamentation. Contemplating the contrast between Words vs. Silence, Caraza asks directly: What cures us, what heals us, what gives us strength, what nourishes us? These questions direct us to the self, but also to the world. Within the captivity of life interrupted, Caraza asks, "What frees us?"

The work of witness through these poems offers answers. Though loneliness meanders through these poems like a river, even within the stillness of solitude and isolation, these poems thrum and reach, each tercet a heartbeat of affirmation and connection. Through incantations and evocations, these poems affirm and hope. Working from Spanish to English, Caraza creates meditative repetition that weaves the two languages, the two parts of her identity into one voice: "With poetry we disperse / times of darkness. / Words that heal / isolated hearts."

Amy Sage Webb-Baza, Ph.D.
Emporia State University

I
Corazón de agua
Heart of Water

Corazón de agua

Corazón de agua, **gira**.
Origen del universo,
borbotones de historia líquida.

Los zafiros de las entrañas de la tierra
se desbordan por doquier.

El **agua** canta en su nacer,
en su recorrido por las arterias,
fuente redonda, chorro de fuerza.

Fuente de vida, ecos lacustres,
centro de la tierra, turquesa líquida.

Con la **corriente** se clava en las grietas,
llena la fuente que sana, que baña,
que cura, que lava el dolor.

Gira, agua, **en mi tintero** y
penetra esta página blanca.

Márcala e inserta tus raíces líquidas,
expande la vida, **fluye**, canta,
corazón de agua, canta, baila, gira.

Chorro de fuerza divina, eco lacustre,
báñame, vibra, **llévate el dolor**.

Heart of Water

Heart of water, **twirl**.
Origin of the universe,
effervescent liquid history.

Sapphires from the bowels of the earth
overflow everywhere.

Water sings as it appears,
as it runs through the arteries,
round fountain, stream of strength.
Fountain of life,
lacustrine echoes,
center of the earth, liquid turquoise.

It penetrates the cracks with a **cascade**,
fills the fountain that cures, that bathes,
that heals, that washes the pain.

Twirl, water, **in my inkwell**, and
penetrate this blank page.

Mark it with your liquid roots,
expand life, **flow**, sing,
heart of water, sing, dance, twirl.

Stream of divine strength, lacustrine echo,
bathe me, vibrate, **take away the pain**.

II
Un cardenal
A Cardinal

Nostalgia

Luminosa promesa:
los rayos exteriores
me alumbran.

Rompen la sigilosa
oscuridad que se expande,
incierto devenir.

La **piel** anhela calidez,
reflexiona sobre
los que ya no están.

Los dañados por este
inesperado mal:
álgidas almas.

Por un instante **el sol**
nos transforma en flores
sembradas en las praderas.

Baña un **bosque** en la memoria:
paraíso aún no perdido:
árbol de vida, devuélvemela.

Antes y después, intermitente luz,
vida y muerte, **eterno retorno**,
nostalgia por lo que no será.

Nostalgia

Luminous promise:
external rays
enlighten me.

They break the stealthy
darkness that is expanding,
uncertain evolution.

Our **skin** craves warmth,
reflecting on
those no longer here.

Those hurt by this
unexpected affliction:
essential souls.

For an instant, **the sun
transforms us** into flowers
sown on the prairies.

It bathes a **forest** in memory:
paradise still not lost:
tree of life, return it to me.

Before and after, intermittent illumination,
life and death, **eternal return**,
nostalgia for what will not be.

Esperanza

Somos tormenta sin destino
dispersos en la eternidad,
giros aislados que no
encuentran otro similar.

Esta fulminante realidad sobrecoge,
nos fuerza a establecernos
en **ciudades virtuales**
de luz artificial y metálicas voces.

Somos una nueva generación
de migrantes, obligados a vivir
entre circuitos y ecos electrónicos,
cubiertos con **endebles** cubrebocas.

Esperanza, toma nuestras manos,
llénalas de **rayos** cristalinos
que se reflejen en los corazones
y saturen **nuestros cuerpos**.

Hope

We are a storm of sans destination
dispersed in eternity,
isolated twists and turns that do not
find their equal.

This sudden reality shocks us,
it forces us to find our way
through **virtual cities**
of artificial light and metallic voices.

We are a new generation
of immigrants, compelled to live
amidst circuitry and electronic echoes,
covered by **tenuous** masks.

Hope, take us by the hands,
fill them with crystalline **beams of light**
that reflect in our hearts
and flood **our bodies**.

Confinamiento

Cinco **sílabas**
para revalorar prioridades.

Nuestra obligación:
ser felices a pesar de todo.

Crear rutinas **dentro
de las rutinas.**

Brillar en la oscuridad
y **el silencio** matutino.

Cuatro paredes donde
nuestra creatividad crece.

La fe se **templa** con
el ulular del viento.

Nos trae alegría abrir
las ventanas,

mirar **el sol** nacer
en el horizonte,

redescubrir la concavidad
del manto nocturno,

titilar con miles
de intermitentes estrellas.

Nueva rutina
en soledad.

Lockdown

Two **syllables**
to reassess priorities.

Our obligation:
to be happy despite everything.

To create routines **within**
routines.

To shine in the darkness
and in the **silence** of early morning.

Four walls where
our creativity is cultivated.

Faith is **tempered** with
the howling of the wind.

We find joy just by
opening the windows,

watching **the sun** emerge
on the horizon,

rediscovering the concavity
of the nocturnal cloak,

shimmering with thousands
of intermittent stars.

New routine
in solitude.

Un cardenal

Se percha en lo que
queda del **invierno**.

Me acecha con su cuello
emplumado y **ojos nocturnos**.

Sigue cada uno de mis
movimientos en la cocina.

Correspondo **en silencio**.

Soy yo quien está perchada
en lo que queda de vida.

Crecen las plumas en lo
que fueron mis brazos.

Me veo a través de la ventana
deslizándome **en la eternidad**.

A Cardinal

It perches on what
is left of **winter**.

It stalks me with its feathered
neck and **nocturnal eyes**.

It follows every one of my
movements in the kitchen.

I reciprocate **in silence**.

I am the one who is perched
upon what is left of life.

Feathers **grow** on what
used to be my arms.

I see myself through the window
sliding my way **into eternity**.

Cada cuerpo

Cada cuerpo: víctima
de esta **tenebrosa palabra**.

Pacientes **en los pisos**
de hospitales llenos.

Contingentes vidas:
humanos, nada más que humanos.

¿Hemos olvidado **nuestra fragilidad**?
o, ¿son los dioses quienes nos han olvidado?

Peleamos por la vida para
no caer en las fosas funerarias.

Miedo a pronunciarte
en voz alta para **no invocarte**.

Dejamos fluir este momento
de aislamiento voluntario

para honrar a todos aquellos
que te has llevado.

Each and Every Body

Each and every body: victim
to this **sinister word**.

Patients **pile up**
in overflowing hospitals.

Contingent lives:
humans, nothing more than humans.

Have we forgotten **our fragility**?
Or is it the gods who have forgotten us?

We fight for life,
to not fall into funerary graves.

Fear of saying your name out loud
so as **not to invoke you**.

We let this moment
of voluntary isolation flow

to honor everyone
you have taken.

Una madre más nos deja

Una madre más nos deja.
La distancia **virtual** es
realidad en algún lugar.

Nada cambiará el **dolor**
de una pérdida tan valiosa,
corazón desgarrado.

Tiemblo ante la noticia,
me pongo de **luto**
desde mi confinamiento.

Recuerdo a mi madre,
viva **en su jardín**
compartiendo azaleas.

Las manos no paran,
otras se van, el dolor
nos acompaña

Another Mother Leaves Us

Another mother leaves us.
The **virtual** distance is
reality somewhere.

Nothing will change the **pain**
of such a powerful loss,
heart ripped asunder.

I tremble before the news,
drape myself in **mourning**
in my confinement.

I remember my mother,
alive **in her garden**
handing out azaleas.

Her hands don't stop,
while others take their leave, pain
is our companion

Con poesía

Con **poesía** disipamos
los tiempos oscuros.

Palabras que sanan
los aislados corazones.

Fluye, poesía, entre
las nubes cibernéticas.

Trae pensamientos curativos,
pequeñas **dosis de alegría**.

Sé la medicina para este corazón sin luz,
para esta **sangre** que aún palpita.

Artificiales pulsaciones como
flores se tatúan en la pantalla.

Como **dulce música** que nos baña,
que nos trae dorada felicidad.

With Poetry

With **poetry** we disperse
times of darkness.

Words that heal
isolated hearts.

Flow, poetry, amidst
cybernetic clouds.

Bring healing thoughts,
small **doses of joy**.

Be the medicine for this heart devoid of light,
for this **blood** that continues to flow.

Artificial pulsations like
flowers are tattooed across the screen.

Like **sweet music** that bathes us,
that brings us golden happiness.

III
Cuervo
Raven

Efecto dominó

Con **la fuerza** del efecto
dominó celebramos:

a los que cultivan
nuestros alimentos,

a quienes nos organizan
la mañana,

a nuestros médicos y enfermeras
en el frente de **batalla**,

a quienes recogen la basura
con estoicos movimientos

y al sol que nos inyecta
dorados sentimientos.

Domino Effect

With the **strength** of the domino effect
we celebrate:

those who cultivate
our food,

those who organize
our mornings,

our doctors and nurses
on the **front lines**,

those who collect the garbage
with stoic movements

and the sun that injects us with
golden emotions.

Prestos a la vida

La fuerza es interna:
solo esa nos mantendrá
prestos a **la vida**.

Nada más que proyectar
pensamientos positivos
dejar la negatividad evaporarse.

Llenar de **color** los ojos,
para que brillen ante esta oscuridad,
dominar **la mañana** gris que nos acecha.

Al salir el sol **por mi ventana**
lo decoro con dorados besos
y manos de refulgente plata.

Prepared for Life

The strength is internal:
only that will keep us
prepared for **life**.

Nothing more than projecting
positive thoughts
letting negativity evaporate.

Filling our eyes with **color**,
so they shine before this darkness,
dominating **the morning** dreariness that stalks us.

As the sun rises **through my window**
I decorate it with golden embraces
and hands of resplendent silver.

Punto de fuga

Reencontramos la vida
en las alacenas y closets.
En las gavetas donde
están los recuerdos olvidados.

Tropezamos con **un amor perdido**.
Una nota borrada por el tiempo.
Una caricia que **se enciende**
al invocarla.

Pieles de pasadas dimensiones.
Punto de fuga en la distancia.
Viento que electrifica
la memoria.

No somos más que estatuas
de bronce que este mal
no puede penetrar.
Seguimos desempolvando **la vida**.

Redescubriéndonos entre miradas,
con un abrir y cerrar de cajas oxidadas.
Los años las han enmohecido y seguimos
siendo **nosotros en la eternidad**.

Vanishing Point

We reencounter life
in cupboards and closets.
In the drawers where
forgotten memories lie.

We stumble over **a lost love**.
A note erased by time.
A caress that **ignites**
when invoked.

Skin of past dimensions.
Vanishing point in the distance.
Wind that electrifies
memory.

We are nothing more than bronze
statues that this evil
cannot penetrate.
We continue dusting off **life**.

Rediscovering ourselves as we gaze,
opening and closing tarnished boxes.
The years have rusted them while we continue
being **ourselves in eternity**.

En la pantalla

Escribir para **justificar**
la mañana, el día, la vida,
para dejar fluir **la energía vital**.

Delicados **aleteos como hojas**
de papel caen al vacío,
no son sino el aliento de minúsculas
criaturas que se esconden
de **nuestros pensamientos**.

Diminutos suspiros, lo que
hemos perdido: **aliento y esperanza**:
sonidos traducidos a caracteres,
con los que escribimos
canciones tristes.

Desde la tinta brotan los rizomas
que llevan la esencia de nuestra
existencia.

En zig-zag **vuelan las ideas**
en la pantalla de luz artificial.

On the Screen

Writing means **justifying**
the morning, the day, life,
to let **the vital energy** flow.

Delicate **wingbeats like sheets**
of paper fall to the void,
they are nothing but the breath of diminutive
creatures that hide
from **our thoughts**.

Minuscule sighs, that which
we have lost: **breath and hope**:
sounds translated into characters,
with which we write
sorrowful songs.

Rhizomes spring **from the ink**
and carry the essence of our
existence.

Zig-zagging **ideas soar**
on the screen of artificial light.

El origen de mi sangre

Mi centro es el medio oeste
donde los pies descansan
hace ya varias décadas.

Donde respiro las **ilimitadas
llanuras** y praderas.

Mas el corazón está enterrado
en el **exuberante follaje**
de los bosques de niebla.

Donde el agua
flota en la atmósfera.

Palpita el origen de mi sangre,
se forman surcos en la piel
al deslizarse **lágrimas negras**.

Duele más **la distancia** con
esta inesperada pandemia.

The Origin of My Blood

My center is the Midwest
where my feet have rested
for several decades now.

Where I breathe the **limitless
plains** and prairies.

But my heart is buried
in the **exuberant foliage**
of the forests of fog.

Where water
floats on the atmosphere.

The origin of my blood pulsates,
furrows are formed on my skin
as **black tears** slide down.

Distance is more painful with
this unexpected pandemic.

En la rama

Copos de nieve sorprenden
la primaveral mañana,
forzada realidad.

Confinada estoy entre
recuerdos y albahaca fresca
que busca el sol.

Me entrego a la **nacarada página**.

Un blanco silencio
cubre la terraza de
personales trazos.

Mientras un petirrojo
se posa en la rama
donde apenas **brota la vida**.

On the Branch

Snowflakes surprise
the spring morning,
imposed reality.

Lockdown contains me amidst
memories and fresh basil
that seeks the sun.

I surrender to the **nacre page**.

White silence
covers the terrace with
personal traces

while a robin
alights on the branch
where **life begins to blossom**.

Cuervo

Cuervo me visita de manera digital
para contarme la historia
del **origen** y destrucción
del universo.

Cómo se transformó en
uno negro al haber sido
expuesto al **fuego** por engañar
a la humanidad.

Las moras **en flor** crecen en el jardín.
Blancas, como el primer cuervo, con
el tiempo serán delicias de **obsidiana**.

Pienso en los que viajan en los metros
cada día, sin máscaras, sin distancia
entre ellos sin saber en lo que
se transformarán.

Raven

Raven visits me digitally
to tell me the story
of the **origin** and destruction
of the universe.

How he became
black upon being
exposed to **fire** for deceiving
humanity.

Flowering blackberries grow in the garden.
White, like the first raven, with
time they will be **obsidian** delicacies.

I think of those who travel on the metro
every day, without masks, without distance
between them, without knowing what
they will become.

IV
Aliento
Breath

Se perchan en tus ráfagas

El viento corre,
lleva la lluvia
en sus entrañas.

Cadenciosa corriente aérea
haces cantar los árboles,
haces llorar el alma.

Te siento en toda la piel,
sutil aliento,
me alimentas.

Las canoras aves
se perchan en tus ráfagas
y elevan **sus voces**
para enterrarse en la tierra.

Divino y terrenal
fuerza y aire
tornado de
corrientes opuestas.

They Perch on Your Breezes

The wind flows,
bearing the rain
in its bowels.

Cadenced currents of air:
you make the trees sing,
you make my soul cry.

I feel you upon all my skin,
subtle breath,
you nourish me.

Warbling birds
perch on your breezes
and elevate **their voices**
to entomb themselves in the earth.

Divine and earthly
strength and air
tornado of
opposing currents.

Elíxir

La medicina perfecta
como elíxir ambarino
que refresca el paladar.

Hierbas y gotas
de lluvia de **la última
tormenta**, mezclo.

Revuelvo un recuerdo
para dejarlo ir.
Al invocarlo **se esfuma**.

Agrego **los suspiros**
provocados por las yeguas
que galopan en las praderas.

Bebo el verde esmeralda,
brillante amanecer,
corazón de agua.

Elixir

The perfect medicine
like an amber elixir
that refreshes the palate.

I mix herbs and
raindrops from
the last storm.

I stir a memory
to let it go.
When invoked, it **vanishes**.

I add the **sighs**
provoked by the mares
that gallop on the prairies.

I imbibe the bright green,
brilliant daybreak,
heart of water.

Aliento

Poderoso **aliento**,
cura el alma y desvía
la oscuridad.

Fortalece la respiración
para seguir viviendo
y lleves a la jungla el corazón.

Jade líquido, envuélveme,
tu exhalación se enrede
en mis brazos.

No hay nada que sea mío
en esta tierra
sólo **mi respiración**.

Inhalation

Powerful **inhalation**,
cure the soul and divert
the darkness.

Strengthen breathing
to remain alive
and transport your heart to the jungle.

Liquid jade, encircle me,
your exhalation becomes entangled
in my arms.

There is nothing that is mine
in this land
except **my breathing**.

Magia

Déjame **vivir** con el encanto
de **este áureo amanecer**
que pinta los pétalos
de las flores en mi ventana.

Sentir eso que dejas
en el aire **a tu paso** y
llena los pulmones
de vainilla y miel.

Efímera magia del amanecer.
Tiempo sin tiempo.

Te evaporas en lo inevitable,
dejando ansiedad para el resto
de las largas horas.
Las escucho desaparecer.

Déjame **tocar lo intocable**
entre los dedos que escriben
la historia que nadie recordará.
Inexistentes **aves de la aurora**.

Efímera magia, envuélveme.
Tiempo sin tiempo.

Magic

Let me **live** in the enchantment
of **this golden sunrise**
that paints the petals
of the flowers in my window.

Feel that which you leave
in the air **in your wake** and
fill my lungs
with vanilla and honey.

Ephemeral magic of sunrise.
Time without time.

You evaporate in the inevitable,
leaving anxiety for the rest
of the long hours.
I hear them disappear.

Let me **touch the untouchable**
between these fingers that write
the story that no one will remember.
Inexistent **birds of daybreak**.

Ephemeral magic, encircle me.
Time without time.

Canción de agua

Se acaba el día
mientras las horas
evaden **la memoria**.

No fuimos tiempo
del amanecer.
Ni **dorada fuerza**.

Cielo **en llamas**,
nuestras manos,
atadas al papel.

Salvaje sonsonete
de invisibles insectos.
Efímera canción de agua.

Song of Water

The day draws to a close
while the hours
evade **memory**.

We were not a time
of sunrise.
Nor **golden strength**.

Sky **in flames**,
our hands,
tied to the paper.

Ferocious cadence
of invisible insects.
Ephemeral song of water.

La inevitable

Amanecer de sangre:
te llevo en la mente,
en las venas.

Palpitas en la bóveda
sin viento, sin aves
que opaquen tu fuerza.

La incertidumbre te acompaña,
las horas vibran en esta caja
celestial **con ritmos de agua**.

La voz de la **nostalgia** me alcanza.
La piel se estremece al escucharla,
aliento **de fuego**.

Un día más comienza,
aleatoria luz se disipa
en la concavidad **eterna**.

Céfiro sentir, el viento del oeste
arrecia, las nubes persiguen
la **inevitable muerte**.

Inevitable

Dawn of blood:
I carry you in my mind,
in my veins.

You throb in the cupola
without wind, without birds
that make your strength opaque.

Uncertainty accompanies you,
the hours vibrate in this celestial container
with rhythms of water.

The voice of **nostalgia** discovers me.
My skin trembles as I hear it,
breath **of fire**.

Another day begins,
fortuitous light dissipates
in the **eternal** concavity.

Zephyr sensation, the wind from the west
intensifies, the clouds pursue
inevitable death.

Viaje

La profundidad del mar nos protege
de la **tristeza abismal**,
no hay viento que nos toque.

Salitre **en las venas** asciende
hasta la superficie que refleja
la huella del viento.

Las ráfagas esgrafían la oscuridad
en el agua, el corazón se inquieta.
Honda melancolía, **lamento de fuego**.

Este viaje nos hace crecer
con **dolor y agonía**.
Las corrientes marinas esperan.

Journey

The profundity of the sea protects us
from **immense sorrow**,
no wind touches us.

Saltpeter **in our veins** climbs
to the surface that reflects
the imprint of the wind.

Its gusts create sgraffito darkness
in the water, our hearts become unsettled.
Deep melancholy, **lamentation of fire**.

This journey makes us grow
with **pain and agony**.
Ocean currents await.

Canto helado

A lo lejos se escucha
la tormenta que desgarra,
congela los sentidos.

La brisa nórdica arranca las aves
de los nidos, destruye la armonía
en la tierra, solo **canto helado**.

Las ramas secas se vuelven **tornados
blancos** en la madrugada de azogue.
No hay sol que resguarde las manos.

Son **estas manos** las que recogen
las huellas de desolación en la nieve,
el agua congelada en el corazón.

Son estas manos las que **escriben**
para salvar **la historia que desaparece**
con cada ventisca de dolor.

Frozen Song

In the distance we hear
the storm that shreds,
freezes our feelings.

The Nordic breeze plucks birds
from their nests, it destroys the harmony
on earth, only **frozen song**.

The dried branches become **white tornados**
in the quicksilver morning.
There is no sun to shield our hands.

These are the **hands** that gather
the traces of devastation in the snow,
the frozen water in our hearts.

These are the hands that **write**
to save **the history that disappears**
with every blizzard of pain.

Palabras

¿Qué nos cura?

Los sonidos de la naturaleza
que nos hacen vibrar
con eléctrico **tremor en la espalda**.

¿Qué nos sana?

Los aromas que tuercen las células
que alcanzan el cerebro
para remover **la tristeza**.

¿Qué nos provee de fuerza?

La voz materna **en la distancia**.
Anhelando tocar su mejilla,
abrazos de nostalgia.

¿Qué nos alienta?

Palabras llenas de **esperanza**
plasmadas en la piel
de esta cibernética mañana.

Voces, luz, aromas
palabras, corazón de agua
a – gua, a – gua, a – gua.

Words

What cures us?

The sounds of nature
that make us vibrate
with an electrical **shiver up the spine**.

What heals us?

The aromas that twist the cells
that reach our brain
and banish **sadness**.

What gives us strength?

The maternal voice **in the distance**.
Longing to touch her cheek,
nostalgic embraces.

What nourishes us?

Words full of **hope**
captured on the skin
of this cybernetic morning.

Voices, light, aromas
words, heart of water
wa – ter, wa – ter, wa – ter.

Silencio

Los **retoños** de fuego
se posan en las ramas
invernales que tiemblan.

No hay exuberante **jade**
que se meza con las
ventiscas nórdicas.

Ocre rugosidad **tintinea**
con el viento y los flamígeros
frutos se esparcen.

En el vuelo se entrelazan
con azules retoños, se miran,
se miden para **continuar el vuelo.**

El agua contenida en los blancos
mantos espera: corazón sometido.
Silencio **hasta la primavera**.

Silence

Sprouts of fire
settle on quivering
wintery branches.

There is no exuberant **jade**
that sways with the
Nordic blizzards.

Ocher roughness **rattles
in the wind** and the flaming
fruit scatters.

On the flight, they intertwine
with blue sprouts, look at each other,
size each other up to **continue the flight.**

The water contained in the white
cloak awaits: subdued heart.
Silence **until spring**.

Lo que nos libera

Es el sonido del alma
entre las hojas que
renacen esta mañana:
poderoso **silencio**.

Compartir la niebla
con las aves matutinas,
humo acuático **que nos rodea**,
alimenta el corazón.

De las hojas nuevas
nace el sonoro
lamento del viento,
arrasa el tiempo.

Nos queda un instante
para disfrutar de la lluvia
en la cara, **la luz** en la piel.
Los pulmones se llenan.

Lo que **nos libera** son
las palabras entrelazadas
con las albas páginas,
sílabas áureas.

Página blanca que
se llena **con musicales
destellos** como dardos,
cargados de luz solar.

What Frees Us

It is the sound of the soul
among the leaves that
are reborn this morning:
powerful **silence**.

Sharing the fog
with the morning birds,
aquatic smoke **that surrounds us**,
it nourishes the heart.

From the new leaves
the resounding lament
of the wind is born,
it obliterates time.

We have only one instant
to enjoy the rain
on our faces, **light** on our skin.
Our lungs expand.

What **frees us** are
the words intertwined
with bright white pages,
golden syllables.

Blank page that
is filled **with musical
sparkles** like darts,
laden with sunlight.

Pide agua

El calor aún no acompaña la luz.
La piel todavía **tiene frío**,
el corazón pide agua.

Las primeras noticias
rebozan de esperanza
la gélida mañana.

Las palabras nos sostienen
en los árboles secos.
Nos mecemos con el viento.

Los caracteres impresos
sanan el dolor que nos
rodea, el canto fortalece.

El calor aún no acompaña la luz.
La piel todavía tiene frío,
el corazón **pide agua**.

Somos ráfagas invernales,
planicies cubiertas de escarcha,
trigo marchito **en los campos**.

La vida renacerá
mientras un petirrojo
aguarda **en las ramas muertas**.

It Wants Water

Heat has not yet joined the light.
My skin, **it is cold**,
my heart, it wants water.

The first news of the day
covers the icy morning
with hope.

Words sustain us
in the dry trees.
We sway with the wind.

Printed characters
cure the pain that
surrounds us, songs give strength.

Heat has not yet joined the light.
My skin, it is cold,
my heart, **it wants water**.

We are wintery gusts,
plains covered with frost,
wheat withered **in the fields**.

Life will be reborn
while a robin
awaits **in the dead branches**.

Una llamarada en las ramas

Se llena de **ríos de tinta**
el papel,
cibernética energía.

Nos enredamos en la página,
perdidos entre palabras
sin rumbo.

Como espinas que se entierran,
que **laceran** la superficie
como si rompieran la piel.

Cantamos el dolor en silencio.
Lo sembramos en **la hoja**.
Plantamos profundos alientos.

Un nuevo camino se vislumbra,
una llamarada en las ramas
saturada de amor.

A Blaze in the Branches

The paper
is filled with **rivers of ink**,
cybernetic energy.

We are entangled on the page,
lost among words
without direction.

Like thorns that are buried,
that **lacerate** the surface
as if tearing our skin.

We sing pain in silence.
We sow it on **the page**.
We plant profound breaths.

A new path is discerned,
a blaze in the branches
saturated with love.

Invernales palabras

Crujen las hojas secas
bajo mis pies
este **atardecer de cobre**.

La **luna menguante** se asoma
cubriendo de alba
los pensamientos.

El viento arrastra
las hojas secas
sin piedad

mientras el sol
me regala
su agonizante sonrisa

y **las praderas** se llenan
de invernales **palabras**:
la luna contiene mi suerte.

Un ave emprende su vuelo
para encontrarse con ella.
Deja un haz de hojas **en el aire**.

Wintery Words

Dry leaves crunch
beneath my feet
this **copper evening**.

The **waning moon** emerges
covering my thoughts
with daybreak.

The wind drags
the dried leaves
mercilessly

while the sun
bequeaths me with
its moribund smile

and **the prairies** fill
with wintery **words**:
the moon contains my fortune.

A bird takes flight
to meet the moon.
It leaves a lightbeam of leaves
in the air.

Pensamientos ocultos

Las vibraciones del agua
revelan los pensamientos
ocultos a nuestra consciencia.

Ignorados pensamientos,
inexistentes secretos.
Las **ondas** los encuentran.

Están sumergidos en las almas
agotadas por tanto engaño,
por gotas repletas de desarmonía.

Las corrientes **arrítmicas**
todavía se expanden en la mente.
Hay ecos lacustres que provocan dolor.

Nos llenamos de fuerza acuática,
corrientes que llevan
la música en su interior.

Nos cobijan.
La nostalgia por lo perdido
inunda el corazón.

Thoughts Concealed

The vibrations of the water
reveal the thoughts
concealed from our consciousness.

Thoughts ignored,
inexistent secrets.
The **waves** discover them.

They are submerged in our souls
worn out by so much deception,
by drops overflowing with disharmony.

Arrhythmic currents
still expand in our minds.
There are lacustrine echoes that provoke pain.

We fill ourselves with aquatic strength,
currents that carry
music inside themselves.

They shelter us.
The nostalgia for what was lost
floods our hearts.

Sólo así

Entre sueños
la infantil ventana:
a través de ella
el pico más alto.

A lo lejos,
inalcanzable quimera,
los dedos delinean
el perímetro de la montaña.

Desde el balcón **onírico**
siento la cumbre nevada,
el **aroma** a pinos
penetrar la piel.

Un sueño donde te miraba:
tu nieve, tu altura:
corazón de agua.
Solo así, te puedo sentir.

The Only Way

Among dreams
the childhood window:
through it
the tallest peak.

In the distance,
unattainable chimera,
fingers draw
the perimeter of the mountain.

From the **oneiric** balcony
I feel the snowy summit,
the **scent** of pines
penetrating my skin.

A dream where I was watching you:
your snow, your height:
heart of water.
That's the only way I can feel you
.

V
Corazón de agua
Heart of Water

Corazón de agua

Corazón de agua, gira.
Origen del universo,
borbotones de historia líquida.

Los zafiros de las entrañas de la tierra
se desbordan por doquier.

El agua canta en su nacer,
en su recorrido por las arterias,
fuente redonda, **chorro de fuerza**.

Fuente de vida, ecos lacustres,
centro de la tierra, **turquesa líquida**.

Con la corriente se clava en las grietas,
llena la fuente que sana, que baña,
que cura, que lava el dolor.

Gira, agua, en mi tintero y
penetra esta página blanca.

Márcala e inserta tus raíces líquidas,
expande la vida, **fluye**, canta,
corazón de agua, canta, baila, gira.

Chorro de fuerza divina, eco lacustre,
báñame, vibra, **llévate el dolor**.

Heart of Water

Heart of water, twirl.
Origin of the universe,
effervescent liquid history.

Sapphires from the bowels of the earth
overflow everywhere.

Water sings as it appears,
as it runs through the arteries,
round fountain, **stream of strength**.

Fountain of life, lacustrine echoes,
center of the earth, **liquid turquoise**.

It penetrates the cracks with a cascade,
fills the fountain that cures, that bathes,
that heals, that washes the pain.

Twirl, water, in my inkwell, and
penetrate this blank page.

Mark it with your liquid roots,
expand life, **flow**, sing,
heart of water, sing, dance, twirl.

Stream of divine strength, lacustrine echo,
bathe me, vibrate, **take away the pain**.

Acknowledgments

Thank you to the editors of literary journals, anthologies and websites, in and on which versions of some of the poems of this volume have previously appeared in: *Revista Literaria Monolito, La Bloga.*

About the Author

Xánath Caraza is a traveler, educator, poet, short story writer, and translator. She is the author of twenty books of poetry and two short story collections. She writes for *La Bloga* and *Revista Literaria Monolito*. In 2018 for the International Latino Book Awards she received First Place for *Lágrima roja* for "Best Book of Poetry in Spanish by One Author" and First Place for *Sin preámbulos / Without Preamble* for "Best Book of Bilingual Poetry." Her book of poetry *Syllables of Wind / Sílabas de viento* received the 2015 International Book Award for Poetry. She was Writer-in-Residence at Westchester Community College, NY, 2016-2019. Caraza was the recipient of the 2014 Beca Nebrija para Creadores, Universidad de Alcalá de Henares in Spain. She was named number one of the 2013 Top Ten Latino Authors by *LatinoStories.com*. Caraza has been translated into English, Italian, Romanian, and Greek; and partially translated into Nahuatl, Portuguese, Hindi, and Turkish.

About the Translator

Sandra Kingery is Professor of Spanish at Lycoming College (Williamsport, PA). Kingery has published translations of two books by Ana María Moix (*Julia* and *Of My Real Life I Know Nothing*) as well as a translation of René Vázquez Díaz's *Welcome to Miami, Doctor Leal* and Daniel Innerarity's *The Future and Its Enemies*; Lawrence Schimel's *A Beard for Two*; and a number of books for Xánath Caraza, including *Hudson, Heartbeat, Balamkú, Without Preamble*, and *Where the Light is Violet*. She has published translations of short stories by Julio Cortázar, Liliana Colanzi, Federico Guzmán Rubio, and Claudia Hernández. Kingery was awarded a 2010 National Endowment for the Arts Translation Fellowship to complete her translation of Esther Tusquets's memoir, *We Won the War*.

DEDICATED TO PUBLISHING RAZA AUTHORS

Somos en escrito Literary Foundation Press is an all Raza-run publishing house based in Berkeley, California, dedicated to promoting Raza writers who express the diverse narratives of our communities. We record Raza realities and histories en escrito to inspire solutions through storytelling, rather than provide mere visibility. Our books aim to break oppressive cycles and call others to action towards a future where our gente not only exist, but thrive. Join our Literary Lucha!

Learn more at www.somosenescrito.com

Other Books by
SOMOS EN ESCRITO
LITERARY FOUNDATION PRESS

Somos Xicanas
Edited by Luz Schweig
Armando Rendón, Jenny Irizary and Scott Russell Duncan (2024)

Abuela Lore
by Isabella Santana (2024)

Chicanofuturism Now! Visions of a Raza Future
Edited by Scott Russell Duncan
Armando Rendón and Jenny Irizary (2024)

Bella Collector Cuentos
by Carmen Baca (2022)

*El Porvenir, ¡Ya! Citlalzazanilli Mexicatl:
A Chicano Science Fiction Anthology*
Edited by Scott Russell Duncan, Armando Rendón
and Jenny Irizary (2022)

Our Grandfathers were Braceros and We Too
by Abel Astorga Morales and Rosa Marta Zárate Macías (2021)

Chicano Manifesto (50th Anniversary Edition)
by Armando Rendón, (2021)

Death Song of the Dragón Chicxulub
by R. CH. Garcia (2021)

*Undesirable—Race and Remembrance:
New & Selected Poems*
by Robert René Galván (2020)

Theorizing Cesar Chavez: New Ways of Knowing STEM
by Armando A. Arias (2020)

Postcards from a PostMexican
by Álvaro Ramírez (2020)

Insurgent Aztlán The Liberating Power of Cultural Resistance
by Ernesto Todd Mireles (2020)

Made in the USA
Coppell, TX
31 March 2024

30753228R00056